IMAGES
*of America*

# CLIFTON AND MORENCI
# MINING DISTRICT

*Silver City, Sept. 20th, '72.*
Editor Borderer:

If not taxing your columns too heavily, I would like to speak through them of the late discoveries of copper mines by Mr. R. B. Metcalf.

About four weeks since he left here for the Rio San Francisco for the purpose of locating copper mines if they could be found.

His trip proved a brilliant success, as he discovered what he believes to be the most extensive mine, and containing the highest grade ore ever found in America.

His expression is "the world renowned Santa Rita is no comparison to it." He undoubtedly is the first white man that ever visited these mines.

Had he have had a supply of provisions with him, he would have remained longer, and more thoroughly prospected the country but his supplies were so limited that on his way back he was three days obliged to subsist on juniper berries. He reports that on one mine there is 100,000 tons of ore that can be obtained without the use of pick or shovel; that it is from 1000 to 3000 feet in width and more than a mile in length. This lode will at no distant day rival the well known Lake Superior mines. There are many other mines in the same locality, though not so extensive several of which show native copper, but to what extent is yet unknown. It is believed that the ore contains gold as the mines have been worked, either by the Aztecs or the early Spaniards and it is known that gold exists in that vicinity. The mines must have been worked ages ago as is indicated by the character of the tools found in them, and large trees are now growing on the debris from the shafts.

Mr. Metcalf started again for these mines ten days ago, taking full supplies and a sufficient number of men to do the required work to secure the location, and to obtain a Patent. Capt. Ward of Detroit, has purchased mines on the "Frisco" to the amount of $30,000 and has men now working them.

The troops under Lieut. Stephenson passed through here to day returning from a scout. They trailed the stock stolen from here some time since by the Indians, to the Tularosa reservation and five men were dispatched to the commander of the reservation, asking him that the stock be given up; the result is not yet known. On their return they crossed a fresh trail of Indians making towards this place.

Great credit should be given the Lieutenant as he has successfully carried out his instructions. I understand that the machinery of the Cibola Company has been released and will at once be put up. The mill from Colorado is expected soon. These will materially add to the prosperity and welfare of the camp.

Yours,
C. M. S.

In one of the first reports of the copper riches of the district, Charlie Shannon submitted this letter to the editor of the Las Cruces, New Mexico, newspaper the *Borderer*, which appeared in the September 28, 1872, edition. In the letter, he talked about the copper discoveries of his uncle Robert Metcalfe and how the trip was "a brilliant success, as he discovered what he believes to be the most extensive mine, and containing the highest grade ore ever found in America." (University Libraries, University of New Mexico.)

ON THE COVER: Heading south to Guthrie, a Morenci Southern Railway train crosses the San Francisco River three miles downriver from Clifton. The Detroit Copper Company's dam and flume provided waterpower for the nearby smelter from 1881 to 1884. It also provided water and powered the pumps for the seven-mile, four-inch pipeline to Morenci, where the new smelter was built in 1884. A trip on the Morenci Southern line, and its five loops, was thrilling for travelers. The railroad had two passenger trains per day, and in 1909, a car with an open observation deck was purchased to enhance the passengers' experience. (Arizona Historical Society.)

IMAGES
*of America*

# CLIFTON AND MORENCI
# MINING DISTRICT

Robert A. Chilicky and Gerald D. Hunt

ARCADIA
PUBLISHING

Published by Arcadia Publishing
Charleston, South Carolina


Library of Congress Control Number: 2015936957

For all general information, please contact Arcadia Publishing:
Telephone 843-853-2070
Fax 843-853-0044
E-mail sales@arcadiapublishing.com
For customer service and orders:
Toll-Free 1-888-313-2665

Visit us on the Internet at www.arcadiapublishing.com

This book is dedicated to our friends Don and Jo Lunt. They have been faithfully committed to preserving the memories and history of the Clifton and Morenci Mining District. Their work with the Greenlee County Historical Society leaves a legacy of civic pride and service. Don is a gifted photographer who has captured and preserved many memories of the district. Jo successfully taught several generations of Clifton and Morenci students. They personify the sense of community and family that we cherish. In this book, we hope to share our gratitude and respect for them. (Don and Jo Lunt.)

# CONTENTS

# ACKNOWLEDGMENTS

Many books, articles, pamphlets, poems, short stories, and songs have been composed about Greenlee County's Clifton and Morenci Mining District. Inspiration for this book arose from conversations, online interactions, friendships, and a passion for the history and culture of these towns and their people. Many of the photographs come from the Greenlee County Historical Society (GCHS) in Clifton and the Arizona Historical Society (AHS) in Tucson. Also, thanks to Bette Pine Antonson (BPA), Anne Baker (AB), Hal Gilliland (HG), Carlos Madrigal (CM), Carl and Patty Moore (CPM), Florencio Navarrete (FN), June Potter Palmer (JPP), Alicia Scudamore (AS), Marlin Treadaway (MT), and Pat Waldorf (PW) for providing pictures and information. Darrin Tenney provided baseball information. Images also come from the personal collections of Robert A. Chilicky (RAC) and Gerald D. Hunt (GDH). Some photographs are within the Public Domain (PD). Thanks also to Ed Gonzalez and Felix Callicotte for community and picture information. We thank the Graham County Historical Society for the use of the William Ryder Ridgway Collection (WRR). Lastly, a special thanks to our families and friends for your words of encouragement, advice, and support. It is our sincere hope that by sharing this rich history, the strength and endurance of the communities will show what hardworking people can accomplish.

# INTRODUCTION

The quest for riches lured many men out west. Some searched for gold in California, while others sought their fortunes mining in Arizona. Begun in the 1870s, these Arizona towns have lived a life that could only be found in a Hollywood script. The area was unsettled and rough. Transportation between the mines and the outside world was challenging. Attacks by Apaches from the nearby San Carlos Indian Reservation were a constant threat to prospectors, freighters, mines, and smelters. Those who first mined and settled had to have courage and fortitude to survive the area's dangerous challenges. The area was first known as the Copper Mountain Mining District and the extent of the riches that waited discovery would soon be realized.

Between 1870 and 1872, Joe Yankie and the Lesinsky, Metcalfe, and Stevens brothers, along with their associates, established the first claims and started mining operations but not without many setbacks, travails, and disputes. The Lesinskys built the first narrow-gauge railroad in Arizona in 1879. First called the Clifton Railroad, the mule-powered Coronado Railroad transported ore faster and safer over the four and a half miles from the mines to the Clifton smelter. A steam locomotive was purchased in 1880. William Church, one of the area's most successful developers, arrived in 1880 and supervised the Detroit Copper Company. He traveled from the Arizona mines to New York City to request financial backing from Phelps, Dodge & Company. James Douglas recommended the investment, and the mercantile company took the risk. The payoff was huge, and it changed the company's direction and identity. Phelps Dodge eventually became one of the world's largest copper producers.

Outlaws and rustlers were common in the early days. In their own special way, they added a sense of danger and drama to the area. One such character was a fellow named Rufus Nephew, but everyone called him "Climax Jim." This nickname came from his favorite brand of chewing tobacco. Jim was always in trouble with the law for such crimes as cattle rustling and larceny. Once, he was arrested for trying to cash an altered check. While in court, and with the check in question on the table nearby, Jim walked over to the table and stuffed the check in his mouth. No one seemed to notice because the lawyers were arguing. When the judge called for the check, it could not be found, and the case was dismissed for lack of evidence. Outlaws Black Jack Christian and Ike Clanton were hunted down and killed nearby. Groups of warring Apaches, including Geronimo, who was born around 1829 near present-day Clifton, and Victorio, led raids on William Church's San Francisco River smelter and other locations, killing a number of smelter men and freighters and threatening the area.

Numerous mining companies operated in the district, holding over 700 claims. The bigger companies were more successful; however, smaller ones still found a way to survive. Eventually, many went out of business or were bought out by the larger companies. With the sale of the Arizona Copper Company to Phelps Dodge in 1921, the district was consolidated under one company and continued producing copper. Gold and silver mines prospered, but copper remained king.

# One

# EARLY EXPLORERS AND IMPORTANT PEOPLE

Exploring and developing an area like the Clifton and Morenci district took a special kind of person. They were characters strong in both mind and body. The first American explorers, soldiers, and prospectors found promising surface mineral deposits and signs of ancient mining, including stone tools and shallow trenching. The quest for gold encouraged many people to search for a rich strike, and copper was not the main objective.

Francisco Vázquez de Coronado is generally considered the region's first explorer while on his quest for the Seven Cities of Cíbola from 1540 to 1542. Don Jose de Zuniga's exploration, originating from Tucson, visited the locale in 1795. Various artifacts were left by these groups, including charcoal drawings, spontoons, and buttons. In 1914, Joe Place found a Spanish sword along the Gila River while helping construct a dam west of Duncan. Initially, he paid no attention to the sword and put it in his toolbox. His father-in-law, George Gamble, noticed the sword's gold inlay, Roman cross, and Knights Templar plume. Local historians agreed that the sword was from the conquistador era.

Originally, the mines were within the boundaries of the San Carlos Indian Reservation. Apaches roamed the area, often taking livestock and provisions or harassing and sometimes killing miners. With the help of the federal government, reservation boundaries were changed, and mining continued to grow.

Ambitious and creative people worked to promote education, improve mining techniques, and develop the towns and businesses. The men who first spotted copper outcroppings and the heavy mineralization of Chase Creek were visionaries. They foresaw a great mining district, and many who gambled on that future watched their dreams come true.

James Ohio Pattie (1804–1851) traveled up the San Francisco River between 1825 and 1826 and collected over 250 beaver pelts. In this illustration from his book, he is wounded by an arrow. (Arizona Oddities.)

Col. James H. Carleton (1814–1873) and his soldiers from the regiment of California Volunteers reported indications of copper deposits in the area. They were patrolling for hostile Indians when they discovered the mineralization along Eagle Creek and Gold Gulch, which led others who had heard the story to the locale for further investigation. (PD.)

Col. King S. Woolsey (1832–1879) and scouts explored Eagle Creek, known as Rio Prieta, in the mid-1860s. They found gold traces and copper outcroppings. A group of prospectors out of Silver City, New Mexico, made the full discovery of the district's riches about five years later, in 1870. (PD.)

Isaac and Charles Stevens, pictured at left, were among the first prospectors to come to the area. In July 1870, they traveled from Silver City, New Mexico, with about 40 men to search for gold along Gold Gulch, one mile west of what would become Morenci. They did not find much gold but found evidence of high-grade copper. After camping there for a few days, they went home to Silver City. Later, they returned to the area and started the Stevens Copper Company, with mines in the Garfield area north of Metcalf. (*Arizona Bulletin Supplement*, 1903.)

James Metcalfe (1824–1910), seated at left with family, and Robert Metcalfe (1825–1905), above right, were instrumental in the early development and success of the district. The brothers are credited with finding signs of copper in the area while serving as scouts for the Army. They recognized that mining the rich copper ore could be highly profitable, and they returned to make formal mining claims. Later, they sold their claims and mining interests to the Lesinsky brothers after a bitter dispute. The town of Metcalf was named for them. (Left, *Desert Exposure*; right, Ted Cogut and Bill Conger.)

Henry Lesinsky (1834–1924), above left, and Charles Lesinsky (1839–1907), above right, were early New Mexico merchants who explored the Clifton district and established claims. Along with the Metcalfe brothers and others, they founded the Francisco Mining Company. The house Henry built in 1874, La Casa Grande on Clifton's Eastside, still stands and is a testament to the commitment and hard work of the early miners. (Left, GCHS; right, University of Arizona Special Collections.)

Baylor Shannon (1858–1924), left, and Charlie Shannon (1851–1928), right, nephews of the Metcalfes, were in charge of the Shannon Copper Company. Along with the copper company, Shannon Mine, Shannon Incline, town of Shannon, Shannon Railroad, and Shannon Hill in Clifton all bear the family name. Baylor later got into the cattle business, and Charlie served as president for the Bank of Clifton and was elected into the Arizona Territorial Legislature. (GCHS.)

Mason Greenlee (1838–1903), for whom Greenlee County is named, was an early miner in the area. He helped start the Greenlee Gold Mountain Mining District. On March 10, 1909, a new county was created from the eastern side of Graham County. The name of the county was debated for some time. The Arizona Copper Company wanted the name to be Colquhoun after its president, while the Detroit Copper Company wanted the name to be Douglas after the president of that company. A compromise was made, and the name Lincoln was selected. However, an Arizona Territorial Legislature bill amended the decision, and the name Greenlee was finalized. Note that Greenlee's name was misspelled on the headstone. (AS.)

L. D. S. Academy, Thatcher.

Born in Ireland in 1849, Henry Hill (seen above at left) came to Clifton in 1878. In addition to being the proprietor of the Coronado Chop House, he opened the United States Hotel and ran a freighting business. In 1899, he purchased land south of Clifton and west of the railroad tracks. It was named Henry Hill's Addition to Clifton. In 1905, he purchased land in the same area, this time east of the railroad tracks, and it was called Hill's New Addition. In 1910, he donated six lots for the building of the Greenlee County Courthouse and jail, which was completed in 1912. (*Arizona Bulletin Supplement*, 1900.)

William Church (1845–1901) is considered the founder of Morenci. He came to Arizona in 1880 when the Detroit Copper Company began mining operations in Joy's Camp. Looking for investors, he traveled to New York City and visited Phelps, Dodge & Company, convincing them to invest in his operation. His courage and tenacity created one of the most important mining enterprises in the world. In 1886, he built the first concentrator in Arizona. (*Denver Republican*, May 26, 1901, No. 10044187, History of Colorado, Denver, Colorado.)

Phelps, Dodge & Company sent Dr. James Douglas (1837–1918) to the mining properties owned by the Detroit Copper Company in order to assess the mines and determine if the company should invest. His report was favorable, and the mercantile company helped finance the operation. He later became president of Phelps Dodge. He was inducted into the National Mining Hall of Fame in 1988. (PD.)

James Colquhoun (1857–1954), general manager of the Arizona Copper Company, started as the company's bookkeeper. He also served as president of the Arizona & New Mexico Railway, built by the company to provide a link to the Southern Pacific Railroad in Lordsburg, New Mexico. He oversaw the building of more efficient concentrating, leaching, and smelting in Clifton. For years after they left the district, he and his wife would send money to community leaders to buy Christmas presents for the children. He was inducted into the National Mining Hall of Fame in 2002. (GCHS.)

Paul Robert Becker, shown at left at the bottom, emigrated from Germany in 1887 and arrived in Morenci in 1889 at the age of 19. He worked for the Detroit Copper Company store and began acquiring land. After a fire destroyed much of the commercial and "recreational" business district of Morenci in 1897, he founded New Town, just south of Morenci. Becker had several mining claims in this area to go along with his 25 businesses. He built an electric light plant for New Town in 1905. (*Arizona Bulletin Supplement*, 1903.)

Delbert M. Potter (1863–1942), originally from Ohio, came to New Mexico at the age of 17. He was a scout for Troop H, 8th Cavalry and also served as deputy US marshal for the Southern District of New Mexico. Around 1881, he began mining in the Clifton and Morenci area. Potter was an advocate for the improvement of roads and, for a time, served as vice president of the Arizona Chapter for the Ocean-to-Ocean Highway Association. This versatile man was also paymaster general of the National Guard of Arizona. (JPP.)

# Two

# NEIGHBORING
# COMMUNITIES

Small communities and camps served numerous mines. They were as important to the area's success as the bigger towns. Some were railroad hubs, agricultural centers, fuel producers, recreational retreats, and smelter sites. Duncan, originally called Purdy, was an important stop along the Arizona & New Mexico Railway between Clifton and Lordsburg, New Mexico. It became an agriculture and ranching center named for James Duncan Smith, an organizer of the Arizona Copper Company. Solomonville, in the Gila Valley, grew because charcoal was made there to fuel the Clifton-area smelters. Charcoal was made from the mesquite tree forests, helping clear vast tracks of land for farming. It is named for merchant Isador Elkan Solomon. The Gila Valley Bank started at Solomonville in 1899. Branches opened in Clifton and Morenci, eventually becoming the Valley National Bank, Arizona's largest statewide bank.

Some communities have been lost to history. Slag Town was in Morenci Canyon below New Town. It was dismantled to make room for the Morenci Southern Railway. Many businesses relocated to New Town, known for saloons, gambling houses, and brothels. Clifton Heights was planned for the ridge west of Chase Creek but never fully materialized. Queen City, with a rowdy reputation, was just north of the Longfellow Incline. Garfield, serving the Stevens mines, was located between Metcalf and Granville. Coronado, a mile west of the Coronado Incline, had a school and store. Oro, three miles upriver from Clifton, supported a smelter and tramway. Silver Basin, west of Stargo, had a post office. Longfellow was at the top of the Longfellow Incline, and Longfellowville was at the bottom. The first Morenci, near William Church's dam on "the Frisco," had a smelter, store, and housing.

Transportation to outlying communities was challenging and required a network of roads, trails, and railways. Most of these communities no longer exist. Economics and the change from underground to open-pit mining spelled their end. In 1910, the combined population of the area neared 18,000, forming one of the largest mining districts in Arizona.

The San Francisco River smelter site, built by William Church in 1881, was about three miles south of Clifton. It was known as Morenci. Origin of the name has never been satisfactorily determined, although several theories have been proposed. The site was attacked by Apaches in April 1882. Their band was divided into four groups: one watched Gold Gulch near Eagle Creek, one guarded the canyon below Church's Camp (previously known as Joy's Camp), another positioned on the mesa above this smelter, and the last group attacked the smelter complex. (AHS.)

The Detroit Copper Company smelter, along the San Francisco River, was operational starting the spring of 1882. In addition to the smelter, the complex had a pump house, boardinghouse, homes, stables, and store. Problems with Indian raids, financial issues, and the distance caused the works to be moved closer to the mines at Church's Camp in 1884. (GCHS.)

The Detroit Copper Company dam, built by William Church between 1880 and 1881, was constructed of quarried rock to back up the waters of the San Francisco River. The dam enabled the Detroit Copper Company smelter to run its blowers with waterpower. By 1884, it was also powering pumps that pushed water via a seven-mile pipeline to the recently completed refinery at "new" Morenci. Two other important dams were built along this river north of Clifton. One was just upstream from Limestone Canyon and provided water power for the Arizona Copper Company smelter in Clifton. The other was built by Dell Potter just north of his ranch, which irrigated his orchards and supplied drinking water to Clifton. (AHS.)

Guthrie, between Duncan and Clifton on the Arizona & New Mexico Railway, was named for John Guthrie Smith, a director of the Arizona Copper Company. The town served as an important rail hub where standard-gauge rails of the Arizona & New Mexico Railway were next to the Detroit Copper Company's narrow-gauge rails. The Morenci Southern Railway, known as "the Corkscrew Route of America" with its five loops, three tunnels, and several bridges, took travelers and freight to Morenci. On the right, an Arizona & New Mexico train arrives from Clifton, and on the left, a Morenci Southern train prepares to travel to Morenci. (David Myrick.)

At the bottom of the Longfellow Incline, the area was known as Longfellowville, with buildings and a water tower. When the Coronado Railroad was completed in December 1879 a mule-powered train carried people up from Clifton to this spot for a dance and celebration. The ride took one and half hours, going primarily uphill, yet only 30 minutes coasting back to Clifton, with the mules loaded onboard. (GCHS.)

Mules and burros helped move ore from the mines to the inclines. The animals were strong and sure footed, a requirement for the steep mountains and canyons of the district. Before roads were built, these amazing animals hauled about everything a miner and his family needed, from building materials and groceries to ore and mine implements. They were also used for transportation between the towns. (GDH.)

About three miles north of Clifton, along the San Francisco River, was the town of Oro. There, the Copper King Mining Company had its smelter, which operated from January 12, 1891, to its closing in 1892. As the bigger copper companies bought out the smaller ones, ore from the Copper King Mines was transported to the Clifton smelters for processing. Today, only the small slag dump on the west side of the river is visible. (GCHS.)

The famed artist Frederic Remington, seated at far right, spent time in the district in 1882. Pictured with him in Oro are, from left to right, Professor Ainsworth; George W. Wells, an early Clifton banker; Ben M. Crawford, the second sheriff elected in Graham County; and Dutch Charlie, camp cook. The group is preparing for a hunting and exploring trip. Remington was not new to the area. In the early 1870s, he placer mined in Gold Gulch for about a year. It was reported that, in a three-week period, his work paid $6,000 in gold. (GCHS.)

High above the east side of Chase Creek, the town of Shannon stood at the top of the Shannon Incline, north of Metcalf. It included a number of residences, a store, and a boardinghouse. The town built a school in 1910. The only way to get to the town was riding up the incline's cable ore cars or trekking up the long, steep trails at the northern and southern end of the mountain ridge. It was an important community for the miners and their families who called it home. (AHS.)

About one mile north of Metcalf, along Chase Creek, was the town of Garfield. One of the main mines in this area was the Alaska Mine, which had ore up to 30 percent copper. The town had access to fresh springwater, plenty of trees, and cool mountain air. A good road was made between the Garfield and Metcalf. (GCHS.)

The housing development of Stargo was built starting in 1938. It provided housing for the influx of mine employees who were coming to the district with their families as the mine transitioned from underground to open-pit operations. The community's name came from the Stargo Silver Belt Mining Company, which mined there during the early 1900s. The headframes for two of the silver mines are pictured, along with the new housing. (GDH.)

In 1914, New Town was a rough place, with altercations, gunfights, and murders as common occurrences. Paul Becker founded it after a fire had destroyed Hell's Half Acre in Morenci. The town was full of saloons, including the Midway Saloon on the right. In 1920, the Tri-State Investment and Leasing Company purchased the town with the promise of improving the area and offering safe investments. (RAC.)

The town of Coronado, at the top of the Coronado Incline, was run by the Arizona Copper Company. In 1910, the town had a population of 200 and supported a mercantile store and school. Edith Greer was the teacher at the school, which had 40 students in 1909. The tracks at the right led east for about one mile, ending at the top of the incline, which was 3,200 feet long and had a drop of 1,100 feet into Metcalf. (GCHS.)

The town of Clifton Heights was initially planned in 1901 and was to be located about two miles west of Clifton. There, it would be close to the Catholic cemetery and near Shannon Junction, where the connector line existed between the Shannon Railroad and the Morenci Southern Railway. Wide streets, a tram to connect Clifton and Morenci, schools, an opera house, and even a courthouse were also planned. With this advertisement from the *Copper Era* on December 26, 1901, shares were sold to raise money for the project. The idea was raised again in 1905 and 1910, but each time funding fell through, and the project was cancelled. (Arizona State Library.)

# *Three*

# EDUCATION

Education has always been an important part of the district. In 1882, the first schoolhouse was built in Clifton on John Ward's ranch, near the mouth of Ward Canyon. The first teacher hired was scared off in Lordsburg, New Mexico, where he was changing trains to travel to Clifton. Having been told that Indians were on the warpath, he went back home to California. A teacher from St. Louis, Missouri, a Mr. Murphy, was then hired to fill the position. He received $30 a month, plus room, board, and laundry. Another early school was on Clifton's Eastside, which was abandoned in 1898 and washed away in the 1905 flood.

The Arizona Copper Company and its manager James Colquhoun took an interest in providing a solid education for children in the area. Colquhoun was known for being a humanitarian. The company wanted to provide services for the miners' families, and mining was becoming complex, so a good education was essential. Over the years, Clifton's schoolchildren enjoyed a number of nice buildings.

Citizens helped out from time to time too. One day, as a teacher and her students were walking back to the North Clifton School by way of the Chase Creek business district, people noticed how poorly the children were dressed. Later, a knock was heard at the front door of the school, and a businessman from Chase Creek presented money collected for the kids.

Morenci's school system started in 1881 with a Miss Davis teaching in a lodging house room. Soon the Detroit Copper Company built a small school near their store. Over the years, at least 11 more modern buildings were constructed. Metcalf had two schools—an elementary school and a high school. When they were closed in the 1920s, the children were sent to either Clifton or Morenci. Many of the outlying areas created their own schools. As many as 25 school districts were established throughout the area, with some being a simple one-room building.

Morenci High School opened in March 1921 and was used until 1949. It had four unique features. There were few stairs inside; inclined ramps led from floor to floor. The building had eight half-floors, with each having its own ground entrance. The assembly hall on the top floor was an amphitheater with the stage and gymnasium in the middle. When basketball or other sports were played, a wire fence was lowered to protect the audience. Lastly, it had a spiral fire escape slide, with a landing at each floor. After the building was vacated, it was sold to Phelps Dodge for $1 because there were no interested buyers. (1972 *Copper Cat*.)

The second Morenci High School was constructed in 1949 and used until 1982. Four classrooms were added in 1954, and the beautiful auditorium at lower left was completed in 1955. The school was built on the site of the old Detroit Copper Company smelter and machine shop. The school's population highpoint was close to 800 students. Many of the seats from the auditorium were moved in 1982 to the new Morenci High School gymnasium in Plantsite and are still being used today as reserved seating. (GCHS.)

Clifton's first high school, built in 1904, was located in South Clifton. Prof. Olaf Halverson was the principal and only teacher. The flood of January 1905 partially demolished the school, and it was decided not to rebuild or even repair the structure. By 1907, it had been completely destroyed by subsequent floods. Until a more fitting school could be built, classes were held in various locations in South Clifton for several years. One of the sites was the Santa Teresa building. In 1907, it was called Clifton Union High School. (GCHS.)

Clifton High School was built in 1912. A broad set of stairs provided access to the second floor, where there was a large assembly room with a stage. The basement was half aboveground, affording ample light in all rooms. The same contractor built this school, along with the Chase Creek, Shannon Hill, and Metcalf Elementary Schools. (GCHS.)

The elementary school at Metcalf was built for $18,000 in 1913. It had six classrooms with every modern amenity. Adjoining the back of the main building was an addition with study rooms. The principal's office was on the upper floor. (GCHS.)

Metcalf High School was built for $26,400 in 1916. Grading the ground for the construction cost $1,160. The school had 20 rooms with the most modern furnishings available. With art as a hobby, the school superintendent had fine copies of famous paintings displayed on the walls. The class of 1920 had the most graduates up to that time, with five. The building was sold in 1940 for $1,000, and some of the bricks were used for construction projects in Morenci. (GCHS.)

The Chase Creek School was opened in December 1912. Enlarged in 1917 to accommodate the growing population of Clifton, it had the modern convenience of drinking fountains on each floor. In its latter years, the school was used by the Catholic Church for classes and dances. The top floor would bounce when a large crowd was dancing. It was demolished in the early 1980s. The original school on this street was known as the Egan School, named for M.J. Egan, the former chief counsel for the Arizona Copper Company. (GCHS.)

The South Clifton School, at right, opened in March 1908, followed by the Clifton High School gymnasium in 1917. This school was built after the new high school was destroyed during the January 1905 flood. Rather than rebuild that school, Henry Hill donated city lots for a new school. For this reason, it was sometimes referred to as the Hill School. The gymnasium was expanded in 1936 with the help of funds from the Works Progress Administration (WPA). (GCHS.)

The North Clifton School was built in 1902 when the Arizona Copper Company pledged $15,000 to help with the educational needs of the community. The cooperative spirit between town and company was a source of pride. Out of respect for the company's manager, the school was also known as the Colquhoun School. The school burned down in 1944. (GCHS.)

The Longfellow School, also known as the Red Brick School, was originally a one-story building. It was officially opened on November 20, 1901, at a construction cost of $22,000. The Detroit Copper Company paid $15,000, and the Arizona Copper Company provided $7,000. When first built, the school had six classrooms, an office, recitation room, and an apartment in the basement for the custodian. The second floor was completed in September 1907, adding four more classrooms. High school classes were also held here for a time. A spiral fire escape slide was built in the 1930s. The roof collapsed in the late 1960s, and the building was condemned and demolished. (GCHS.)

The Shannon Hill School opened in December 1912 and was used until 1923. The original plans called for a one-story building, but the growing school-age population necessitated a second floor. An earlier schoolhouse on Shannon Hill was known as the Bennie School, named for J.W. Bennie, who was the general manager of the Shannon Copper Company. (GCHS.)

Viewed from this B Hill neighborhood are the Fairplay School buildings on the left. The structure on the right was built in 1912. It first housed offices for the timekeeper, office staff of the smelter, metallurgical clerks, and assayers of the Detroit Copper Company. The structure on the left was built in 1916 as the Manual Training and Domestic Science building. In later years, this building was utilized for more classrooms and the school band room. Across the elevated walkway is the Humboldt School, which was built in the 1950s. It had seven classrooms, a library, and a lunchroom, which also served as the cafeteria for the other schools. The school was unusual, with the playground being on the roof. In the middle distance is Coronado Elementary, right below the Morenci Club. (MT.)

On a day off, teachers of Metcalf enjoyed spending time together siteseeing and having fun around town. Mining camps tended to pay teachers more than other communities. One of the teachers, Reba Scott, took this picture of her fellow educators in 1920. She received $140 a month for teaching second grade. (AB.)

A teacher and children of the Chase Creek School pose for this 1914 class photograph. The children of this school enjoyed a big playground, even after the schoolhouse was expanded in 1917. (RAC.)

# *Four*

# SPORTS AND LEISURE

Residents' hard work was rewarded with many sports and recreational opportunities. Activities included trips up the Coronado Trail to enjoy the cool mountain air, fishing trips up and down the San Francisco and Gila Rivers, riding inner tubes down the river, camping and cookouts, hunting, horseback riding, and numerous other favorite pastimes. The Coronado Trail, which was Highway 666, was also known as the Devil's Highway. Outdoor barbecue and hand-cranked ice cream were very popular. In the early days, the saloons and gambling houses were busy day and night with miners freely spending their well-earned wages.

The towns could be quite cosmopolitan, and the clothing stores carried the latest fashions. In the midst of rough and dirty mining operations, people often dressed to rival those in the bigger cities. Ladies sometimes carried calling cards that could be left in a slot by the door if their friends were not home at the time they visited. When the opera houses and theaters were built, they brought in nationally recognized and world-renowned entertainers. These events were very popular and greatly appreciated. In 1910, world-famous opera singer Ellen Beach Yaw came to Clifton and performed at Prettyman's Opera House. In the early days, Clifton boasted the Royal, Princess, and Empire Theaters, while Morenci enjoyed the Star and Royal Theaters. People in Metcalf were entertained with dances, orchestras, magicians, and moving pictures at Juarez Hall.

Sports have always played an important and popular role in Clifton and Morenci. Bowling leagues, adult softball, company-sponsored baseball teams, football, basketball, and even the game of cricket found its way into the community. Soccer, which the men from England and Scotland called football, was introduced by athletes from foreign countries who had come to work locally. Youth, high school, and adult sports teams were state powers and consistently competed for championships. Mining town teams had a reputation of being well coached, hard-nosed, and highly competitive—a reputation that followed the teams as they traveled to compete in other communities. The rivalry between Clifton and Morenci High Schools was intense and often pitted friends and family against one another. In reality, athletes and their families worked for the same company, went to the same churches, shopped in the same stores, and fished and swam in the same river. Fellow townspeople worked hard and played hard as well.

The 1915 Clifton High School girls' basketball team is shown posing for their team photograph next to the Arizona & New Mexico Railway freight depot. They enjoyed a successful season, playing teams from around the region. (GCHS.)

By 1929, the Cherry Lodge recreational area near Granville had opened for business. Named for the wild cherry trees that grew in the area, the site had a store and cabins. Meals were sometimes available, and patrons ate at the proprietors' table. Whether it was having a family picnic or enjoying time off in the mountains, this area was a favorite place for people to visit. Many anglers came here to dig worms for their fishing trips to Honeymoon Campground and Upper Eagle Creek. Church and school activities were held on-site throughout the years as well. Here, Angelina Rios is on a school field trip around 1948. (FN.)

Many of the mining companies in Arizona and New Mexico had baseball teams. Competition between the teams and companies was heated at times. Personal and company pride, not to mention money, were at stake. Star players like Chief Myers (Arizona Copper Company) and Bob Harmon (Detroit Copper Company) went on to play in the Major Leagues. On April 29, 1909, the *Copper Era* announced an upcoming baseball series between Clifton and Bisbee. (Arizona State Library.)

# Base Ball!

## CLIFTON
vs.
## BISBEE
# 3-GAMES-3

**Saturday Afternoon**
**Sunday Morning**
**Sunday Afternoon**

Saturday Afternoon Game Called at 3:30
Sunday Morning at 10
Sunday Afternoon at 3:00

Bisbee has one of the strongest professional teams in the Southwest, having all salaried players. Clifton will have up her best men.

**Come out and help the Boys Win**

Admission 50c.

As described in the *Copper Era* of February 23, 1905, the Morenci YMCA played the University of Arizona in basketball. It was the first-ever game for the university team, winning 40-32. The game was held in the gymnasium portion of the Morenci Club. The university did not have many options regarding who they played in the early days, so they scheduled games against the surrounding communities. (Arizona State Library.)

A good sized audience saw the Morenci basket ball team go down to defeat before the slim youngsters from the University of Arizona on Wednesday evening of last week. The battle was a hard one but the superior team work of the visitors turned the scale in their favor.

The football field for Morenci High School, affectionately known as "The Hill," was a unique source of pride. It was built on the Detroit Copper Company slag dump in 1909. Visiting teams were intimidated playing there because the smelter's sulfur smoke sometimes settled on the field, causing players to cough and gasp for air. Morenci athletes could be intimidating too, regularly fielding some of the best teams in the conference and the state. Morenci won the state football championship in 1976. (GCHS.)

The New Italian Band in Morenci was a town favorite for many years. They performed at many social events, outdoor concerts at the plaza, and funerals, where they played favorites of the deceased and their families. The Mexican population also had musicians perform at social events and funerals. Men at the front of the funeral procession would fire their pistols and shotguns in the air to ward of evil spirits as they marched to the gravesite. (GCHS.)

Burro races in Clifton were always a popular event. The burro was a loyal animal with a wide range of uses, including packing such items as lumber, groceries, firewood, and ore. Many spent most of their lives pulling ore cars and living in the mine tunnels, where there were underground stables. Here, they are helping bring fun and enjoyment to everyday activities. (WRR.)

Cricket matches were often played on Clifton's Eastside tennis court. Employees of the Arizona Copper Company brought the game with them from England and Scotland. Even Norman Carmichael, the company's president, played in a few matches and showed off his skills. In August 1908, the Clifton Cricket Club traveled to Santa Monica, California, to take on some of the best clubs on the West Coast. The game was very unusual for the local people watching the matches, but they learned to enjoy it. For the players, it brought a piece of familiarity from home. (GCHS.)

The ball field in Morenci was built on top of the Detroit Copper Company slag dump and mill tailings. The first baseball game on this field, between Clifton and Morenci, was held on May 23, 1909, with Clifton winning 3-2. This is an action shot from 1914. Many of the baseball athletes played for their mining companies. Others were only on the company payroll as members of the baseball team. Long hours and tiring work shifts did not deter men from hours of practice and road trips. (RAC.)

Clifton High School's Stanton Stadium is being used for a Boy Scout jamboree in 1947. It was the home of many memorable football and track teams, as well as special events. The 1936 stadium dedication honored A.C. Stanton, who was then mayor of Clifton. The 1959 and 1960 high school teams were state champions, with both teams going undefeated. The author's 1982 junior high team also posted an undefeated record. In 1985, the stadium was the site for the last Copper Ingot game between Clifton and Morenci. For a time, baseball was also played on this field. (AHS.)

Sports rivalries between Clifton and Morenci High Schools were very competitive and sometimes heated. Sporting events between the schools were well attended and brought out the best in athletic competition. From 1938 to 1985, the schools played for the highly prized Copper Ingot trophy during the annual football game. This 1981 photograph was taken during the last rivalry game on "The Hill." Morenci Wildcat Joey Merino (No. 83) tackles his cousin Clifton Trojan Armand Merino (No. 12). Clifton won 13-6. (Morenci High School *Copper Cat* staff.)

In the shadows of mining operations, people participated in various sporting events, such as this tennis match. Note the line judge, spectators, and the covered seating at the court's edge. Clifton and Morenci competed in tournaments on a regular basis, and even the company superintendents showed an interest by awarding prized trophies to the winning teams. (GCHS.)

Destinations along the Coronado Trail were favorite getaways for many area residents. Places such as Alpine, Springerville, Big Lake, East Fork, and Luna Lake, along with the many campgrounds, were very popular. The White Mountains were a perfect place to escape the summer heat with picnics, camping, fishing, hunting, or just taking a scenic drive. In the fall, the changing leaves were beautiful. When the snow fell, families could play in the winter wonderland and cut down a Christmas tree. Here, Darlyne Pine enjoys a day in the mountains in late 1947. (BPA.)

Town festivals were a time of fun and friendship. Whether it was playing a favorite game, listening to a band in the plaza, or visiting the many vendors, all who participated enjoyed these events. The food concessions, with their wide range of international cuisine, were a big draw as well. Here is such a day in Morenci in 1914. (RAC.)

Since there was very little level ground around Morenci, children would play baseball on any flat surface they could find. Sometimes that meant playing among trains and the busy area of the Detroit Copper Company store, which was one of the few large, flat areas in town. (GCHS.)

Another popular place was the Mule Creek area in the mountains east of the district, which provided an escape from the mining camps with many hunting, fishing, and camping spots. Needles Eye was the main attraction on the winding road. When the road was built in 1922 for $120,000, it tunneled through this huge rock formation. Sadly, the rock was removed to accommodate roadway expansion in 1976. (Arizona Historical Society, Irwin Brothers Photograph Collection, PC 182_B1_F15_B.)

Bowling leagues were a welcomed pastime for many people, providing friendly competition among friends. The bowling alley in the basement of the Morenci Club had four lanes where teams could compete while their families looked on. The club also had excellent pool and snooker tables. From left to right are Dali Lancieri, Red Sprouls, Cooter Ramsey, Herschell Gilliland, and Walter Young. (HG.)

Local historian Don Lunt is standing at far left with his Boy Scout troop at Clifton's Stanton Stadium in 1947. Scouting offered young men a safe and wholesome group to belong to. Girls could be members of the Brownies, Girl Scouts, Rainbows for Girls, and Job's Daughters. Young people were encouraged to join organizations that promoted life skills, patriotism, and positive social interactions. (GCHS.)

Football teams from Clifton High School were known throughout the state as hard-hitting squads. In December 1913, Clifton shared the state football championship with Phoenix High School. Both teams were undefeated, but Clifton had a wider margin of victory in its games than Phoenix did in its against common opponents. Clifton tried to schedule a game with Phoenix to settle the score, but it could not be arranged. The Phoenix team had no desire to play Clifton, and the *Copper Era* newspaper suggested that they were afraid they would lose, so the schools shared the championship. (GCHS.)

The Morenci Club was a center of community life in town. It opened on April 28, 1902, and dances, social events, mining business, club meetings, and even sporting events were held here. There was a billiard and pool room, double bowling alley, baths, a library and reading room, a large card, checker and chess room, and a gymnasium. A lavish dance was held here once a month and quite often the US Military Band from Fort Grant, Arizona, came to provide the music. In later years, the bowling alley was expanded to four lanes, and the Royal Theater operated here for a time. (RAC.)

The area just southeast of Morenci Canyon was the site of a golf course laid out in the tailings. The new reduction works would be built here over the next several years, but at this time, the area was still wide open. As early as 1914, plans were discussed to build a country club here. The site was selected because it was accessible from the three towns, the views of the surrounding mountains and Chase Creek Canyon to the right were spectacular, and it had plenty of room for expansion. This area became known as Bunkers. The country club never materialized. (GCHS.)

Some clubs and organizations held meetings in the abandoned underground mines, taking advantage of the seclusion. Many of the deserted tunnels went hundreds of feet into the mountain, and the exact meeting location was a closely held secret, adding to the club's exclusiveness. One of these organizations was the Morenci Dirty Club, which was exclusively for men. (RAC.)

Fourth of July celebrations were favorite events. Many activities were held, and people loved showing their patriotic side. Note the Cliff Jail in the distance does not have an entryway building. (GCHS.)

Even with the San Francisco River flowing through town, the building of a city swimming pool on Clifton's Eastside was a welcomed addition in 1927. It offered families a central location to enjoy their day and feel safe doing it, as seen in this Fourth of July celebration that year. The water for the pool was supplied from a hot spring located nearby. Water was piped into the middle of the pool from underneath and sprayed into the air to help cool the water. (GCHS.)

The Clifton Tennis Club, sponsored by the Arizona Copper Company, competed regularly with the Morenci team and in tournaments throughout the state. The mining companies were proud of their sports teams. Here, Norman Carmichael (far right), general manager of the Arizona Copper Company, poses with the team on the Eastside tennis court with a trophy won at a recent tournament. Tennis has been played in the district at a high level throughout the years with many individual and team state championships won by Morenci and Clifton High Schools. (GCHS.)

The Morenci Pool, built in 1953, offered a place for families to enjoy hot summer days, along with Teen Night dances for the young people in the evening. The pool was built near the site of the former Detroit Copper Company smelter and the ruins of the Arizona Copper Company's No. 6 concentrator, known as El Molino. Sounds of laughter, music, and kids' shouts could be heard echoing off the surrounding hills all over town. (GCHS.)

The 1925 Morenci High School boy's basketball team was a tough bunch. Pictured are, from left to right, (first row) Placido Pelusi, George Bazzetta, John Bazzetta, and Pete Marietti; (second row) John Marietti, Guido Cislaghi, Coach Trinko, Frank Ruedas, and Phillip Gualdoni. Cislaghi went on to be a coach, educator, and administrator at Clifton schools for 34 years. The newer gymnasium in Clifton is named in his honor. (GCHS.)

The Arizona Copper Company built a library in Clifton in 1898. The library affirmed the company's commitment to learning as a place for relaxation and education. The building later was used as a mercantile. (PW.)

The 3 Way Drive-In Theatre opened in 1954, with Claude E. Davis as the first owner and manager. Later, he sold it to the Long Theatre chain, and Raymon Parsons became the manager. The structure of this screen was unique because it housed the manager's apartment. A play area in front of the screen entertained children so their parents could enjoy the movie. (PW.)

Innovation in mining towns was not isolated to mining operations. The Morenci Athletic Field is shown here on October 19, 1935, in one of the first football games played at night in Morenci. The first night game was played on September 28, 1935, when Morenci hosted Lordsburg, New Mexico. Outweighed by 20 pounds per player, Morenci played tough, with Lordsburg winning 7-0, scoring in the final minutes. (GCHS.)

# Five

# CLIFTON

Clifton emerged from Goulding's Camp, named for Eugene Goulding, who was an early miner. In February 1870, Joe Yankie located the Arizona Central Mine and filed the first claim in the district. Traveling from Silver City, New Mexico, in the summer of 1870, Robert Metcalfe and the Stevens brothers were among the first men to aggressively prospect the district. Returning in 1872, the Metcalfe brothers partnered with New Mexico merchants Henry and Charles Lesinsky. Joining with others, they formed the Francisco Mining Company in 1873, the same year Clifton was founded. As the mines grew, they reformed as the Longfellow Mining Company in 1874. Henry was the controlling partner. Their Longfellow and Metcalf mines were among the districts richest. Crude adobe furnaces were built along Chase Creek at the Stone House. Later that year, a replacement smelter was built at the confluence of Chase Creek and the San Francisco River. This location became the center of Clifton, which grew along the river and up Chase Creek. Henry built his large home on the Eastside, and it was known as La Casa Grande. There have been several theories on the origin of how the town was named, but the debate continues.

Clifton needed a laundress, so Henry returned to Silver City and hired an older woman, Dona Juanita. As the camp's only female, she worried that miners would get the wrong idea. Henry hung a sign over her door that said, "No admittance here except on laundry business." He also provided her with guns and provisions, as she ran a much-needed business. Her nephew Pedrito came with her as a guide and protector, and he helped with the cooking.

German immigrant Gallus Metz arrived in 1882. He acquired 160 acres in the wide open area south of the smelter. Known as Metz's Flats, his land was resold for $1,000 in 1891 and used for agriculture. Henry Hill later sold lots in this area, and it became known as Henry Hill's Addition to Clifton. In the early 1900s, the Shannon Copper Company built a refinery on Cemetery Hill, along with homes, a school, and a church, and the area became Shannon Hill. Many mine managers lived in North Clifton. It had an opera house, school, and stores. Chase Creek's Copper Avenue and Eastside's Conglomerate Avenue had numerous "dens of iniquity." The rough reputation came from gunfights, murders, and robberies, and for a time, outlaws ruled Clifton. Through dogged leadership, Clifton became a nice town to live in.

On August 9, 1873, the *Borderer* brought the announcement of a new mining camp called Clifton. With the formation of the Gila and Francisco Copper Mining Companies, mining operations sprang to life, but not without disputes, as was common in fledgling mining companies. The name of the Gila Copper Mining Company was changed to the Longfellow Copper Company on May 1, 1874. By 1905, Clifton had become a thriving community. On the left is a residential area, with the Shannon Copper Company store near the bridge. On the right is the Arizona

Copper Company smelter and the Eastside. The baseball field on the right was the site of many memorable games and a good spot for a circus to set up while in town. For a time, Eastside was known as Old Town. The San Francisco River is flowing like a gentle stream. It shows no signs of the raging river it could become during the many floods that devastated the town throughout the years. (University of Arizona Special Collections.)

The Clifton Armory in South Clifton was built in 1909. It served as the home for Company F, 1st Battalion, 11th Infantry of the National Guard of Arizona Territory, as well as one of the opera houses. Town meetings, dances, and basketball games were also held there. The parade field for the soldiers was across the railroad tracks in front of the building. When the military unit moved to Snowflake, Arizona, in 1914, the building was converted into 12 three-room apartments. (GCHS.)

In 1901, with the continued efforts to make life tolerable for the people in the midst of smelting operations, the Arizona Copper Company built a 50-foot stack on top of the mountain 250 feet above the reduction works at the Chase Creek/San Francisco River junction. A 200-foot horizontal tunnel was bored into the mountain to funnel smoke and dust to a vertical shaft below the stack. (GCHS.)

The Clifton Post Office, which was located just north of the old Arizona & New Mexico Railway station, was located right on the edge of the street, and at times, its location caused traffic jams. Driving skills and patience were put to the test for motorists. Tommy Sidebotham was a well-known, long-serving Clifton policeman who directed traffic for many years at the nearby intersection during the heavy congestion of the mine shift changes. Drivers who broke the 15-miles-per-hour speed limit would face Sidebotham's wrath. (WRR.)

The Chase Creek district continued to be vibrant area throughout the years. This intersection was a social and commercial hub with numerous businesses, including J.C. Penney, the farmer's market, Fernandez Mercantile, El Rey Bar, El Charro Restaurant, and Western Tavern. The three gentlemen are standing in front of the Western's doors. (GCHS.)

53

Opened on September 11, 1913, the Hotel Reardon was constructed under the direction of J.L. Morris, with material provided by the Clifton Lumber and Improvement Company. It had hot and cold running water, which was not common in those days, and each room had a call bell to the front desk. The basement had two rooms for traveling salesmen to display their products, a large dining room able to accommodate up to 50 diners, a kitchen, and a storeroom. (GCHS.)

As the population of the towns grew, it was determined a bigger railroad station was needed. The Arizona & New Mexico Railway passenger station was opened with much fanfare on October 21, 1913. The building was constructed by the firm of Mayfield & Shaw and had ample room for both inbound and outbound passengers. In November 1939, the station was remodeled, and the Coronado Inn, a popular restaurant and bar, opened for business. The restaurant served some of the best meals in town. The second story had a large dance floor and wedding dances were held here, with music provided by local bands. (GCHS.)

In the 1940s, South Clifton was a busy part of town. Residents enjoyed comfortable homes, while being within walking distance of schools, shopping, and church. (GCHS.)

The right half of the Arizona Copper Company general office was constructed in 1904. The left side was added in 1910 to house the offices of the Arizona & New Mexico Railway. When the cornerstone was laid on June 5, 1904, a newspaper and a short history of the company were placed within a time capsule inside the stone. (GCHS.)

In this 1914 view of Clifton looking down Chase Creek toward the Arizona Copper Company smelter, the Chase Creek School is visible at center in the distance, and the winding, steep road to Morenci is on the right. (RAC.)

Shown in the 1950s, Riley's Drugstore on Clifton's Eastside was remodeled throughout the years and was heavily damaged during the 1983 flood. When Pete Riley was starting his business, he pushed a peanut roaster and popcorn machine around town, selling his products door-to-door. He sold homemade candy at his store, and on Sundays, he offered enchilada dinners. (WRR.)

The Shannon Hill cemetery was moved to a Ward's Canyon site in 1909. The graveyard had fallen into disrepair, so it was decided the red hills of the canyon would be a fitting location. The remains of 26 Chinese who had died after coming to the district were shipped to China for burial. (GCHS.)

Floods through Clifton, like the one shown in this view looking toward North Clifton, were very devastating. Frequently, the residents had little warning to seek high ground. The river swept through town destroying everything in its path, leaving the residents to wait for the waters to recede in order to clean and rebuild. (WRR.)

The Clifton Hotel on the Eastside was a great place to stay for people visiting the town. The owner of the hotel, Sam Abraham, ran a successful business and a true gem. In 1907, a three-story addition was made to the back of the hotel to accommodate the men who worked at the Arizona Copper Company across the river, as they desired to be more centrally located. Another addition was constructed in 1911. (GCHS.)

Local businessman Dell Potter, a member of the Ocean-to-Ocean Highway Association, helped sponsor the 1912 coast-to-coast road race from Los Angeles, California, to New York City to determine the best route across the country. The race came through Clifton, and some of the cars used in the event are parked in front of the Clifton Hotel. To the right of the hotel is the Gila Valley Bank and Trust, which became Valley National Bank, the largest bank in Arizona. (GCHS.)

The Arizona Copper Company No. 4 concentrator was tested on April 3, 1900, and was fully operational about 10 days later. This concentrator processed ore exclusively from the Metcalf Incline. There were 33 Frue vanners processing ore in this facility. (GCHS.)

In this view looking north along the San Francisco River, the little-known Clifton Northern Railroad runs along the riverbank. Delbert Potter built the railroad, a line extending north from the Arizona & New Mexico Railway turntable to North Clifton. There, at the ore bins, it connected with the New England and Clifton Copper Company rails to the tramway at Evans Point and the Copper King tramway and smelter at Oro. The ore cars were powered by mule and man. The Shannon refinery handled most of the ore. (GCHS.)

In 1901, the Shannon Copper Company built a smelter in Clifton, about seven miles south of Metcalf, to take advantage of the San Francisco River's water for refining purposes. Even though it was a good distance from the mine, it was very close to the railroad leading out of Clifton. Soon, this location would be a bustling section of town, with smelting and family life being closely intertwined. (GCHS.)

The Arizona Copper Company store on Chase Creek was just north of the Sacred Heart Church. The company built several stores around town in order to meet the needs of the people. They also built a store in South Clifton, near the baseball field. (GCHS.)

Built in 1901, this structure originally was the Young and Clemmons Drugstore. The Shannon Copper Company bought it in 1905 to use as their company store. Like most stores owned by mining companies, people often purchased goods on credit, with wages to be deducted from their next paycheck. The section on the right was constructed first, and in 1907, the section on the left was added to house the dry goods department. (GCHS.)

The San Francisco River has many areas with natural hot springs. The section of river between the train station and the Eastside is one such place. In 1928, Guy L. Frazer of El Paso, Texas, built the Clifton Mineral Hot Springs and Bath House for $30,000. Water from the hot springs was fed directly from the river to the bathhouse, which became a favorite place for people to enjoy its natural healing properties. (GCHS.)

To meet the needs of the ever-growing population, the bridge on the right was built into South Clifton for foot traffic and wagon use. The railroad bridge is also seen in this photograph from 1905. Note the third rail for the line to accommodate standard- and narrow-gauge trains. The Arizona Copper Company hospital, seen on the left, was built in 1900. In 1902, a morgue and obstetrical ward were added, and in 1903, the second building was constructed. The hospital was damaged beyond repair during the 1983 flood and was taken down soon after. (GCHS.)

The smoke-choked area of the Arizona Copper Company works was not a very pleasant place for residents and workers. These conditions were typical of mountainous mining towns, as the smoke tended to settle in the low areas. To upgrade smelting techniques and improve air quality, the company built a new smelter about two miles south of town. The smelter complex shown here was shut down for good on January 1, 1914. (GCHS.)

The bridge in North Clifton into Patterson's Addition was originally located downriver, connecting the Eastside to the reduction works area. After the 1916 flood, the bridge was moved to this site to replace a footbridge that had been destroyed, but it too was demolished during the 1983 flood. (GCHS.)

Patriotism was high when the United States entered World War I, and many men signed up to go "over there" and serve their country. Here, an Arizona & New Mexico Railway train is surrounded by well-wishers as they see the men off to military training camps on May 27, 1918. A Becker-Franz Company truck, which was a prominent business in Clifton, is seen at lower left. (GCHS.)

Conglomerate Avenue on Clifton's Eastside was a bustling section of town. These three men are pictured in front of C.F. Pascoe's funeral home on the left, with the always busy Central Hotel next door and the Eagle Restaurant across the street. George and Julia Hormeyer owned and operated the hotel. The first-floor walls were constructed with slag, making the hotel extremely sturdy. (GCHS.)

Copper Avenue, later called Chase Creek, was as rugged and dangerous as many of the more famous Western business districts. Outlaws frequented the numerous saloons, and working girls plied their trade. Businesses thrived here as well. The BBB store at center was owned by Rafael Valdez and his brother-in-law Tomas Bianes. In April 1902, Valdez was made general manager of the Katz Store in Metcalf, and the name transferred to the new location. (GCHS.)

A funeral procession through Chase Creek passes in front of the Arizona Copper Company store (center) and the Sacred Heart Catholic Church around 1905. The church, made from stone, was built at this location in 1917. It remains active as an important part of spiritual and community life. (GCHS.)

There were many ranches in the surrounding mountains and valleys of the district. Cattle drives through Clifton were a common sight as ranchers drove their stock to the railheads so they could be shipped to market. (GCHS.)

This view of Clifton's Eastside shows Lesinsky's La Casa Grande, one of the town's tennis courts, and the Clifton Hotel. Both tennis and cricket were played on this court, and many social events and dances were held at this site. During the dances, music would echo off the canyon walls. (GCHS.)

Clifton was the end point for the Arizona & New Mexico Railway. For the return trip to Lordsburg, New Mexico, trains had to be reversed, so the locomotives would be spun around manually on this turntable, just north of the passenger station. (GCHS.)

Built by the Arizona Copper Company in 1898, this is one of the most recognizable buildings in Clifton. The first floor housed the library and post office, and on the second floor was a Masonic Lodge. The library hall provided a venue for company socials. In 1916, the company announced the drug department of its store would move into the building, and later it became the Clifton branch of the Phelps Dodge Mercantile Company. (GCHS.)

Greenlee County was created on March 10, 1909. Initially the courthouse was in a local tavern in the Chase Creek district of Clifton. Construction and the location of the courthouse and jail was hotly contested. Building was delayed by lawsuits over raised residential rents and cost. A vote in 1910 gave assurances the construction would "not cost the taxpayers a single cent," according to the November 4, 1910, issue of *Copper Era*. Another obstacle was a push to have a station or platform built on the Arizona & New Mexico Railway track in Hill's Addition to make it easier for people who had business at the courthouse. There was also a proposal to have the courthouse and jail on the Eastside. Construction finally began in late 1911 based on the designs of Elmer C. Heck of Clifton. County officials moved into the new facility on September 1, 1912. (GCHS.)

This photograph shows Clifton in 1913 shortly after the train station and freight depot (both at lower left) were completed. The company built a railroad spur bridge, angling to the right, to get material to the construction site of the Arizona Copper Company manager's Eastside residence. A slag wall on the east side of the river was built to protect the house. (GCHS.)

In 1913, the Arizona Copper Company completed a new smelter south of Clifton, which greatly improved air quality in the middle of town. The Arizona & New Mexico Railway provided a special train to transport workers between the Clifton passenger station and the smelter. The company was sold to Phelps Dodge in 1921. The smelter shut down for several years after the sale, then resumed operation into the 1930s. In later years, the smelter stack was a landmark and one of the first sights people saw as they entered town. The stack was demolished in 1997. (GCHS.)

This 1916 photograph was taken following a fire that destroyed the old Arizona Copper Company reduction works, located at the confluence of Chase Creek and the San Francisco River. It occurred when workers were striking against the company, and both sides accused the other of starting the fire. The plant had been decommissioned in 1914 and was no longer producing copper. (GCHS.)

Here is a view of South Clifton, also known as Hill's Addition, in the 1930s. The Shannon Copper Company smelter has been removed from the south side of Shannon Hill. During Prohibition, officials would dump illegal alcohol into the trench on the left so it would flow to the river. Guards were stationed along the trench to prevent people from salvaging the forbidden liquid. (RAC.)

An Arizona & New Mexico Railway train is decorated for a Cinco de Mayo celebration in Clifton, just north of the engine house at the Arizona Copper Company reduction works. The mining companies routinely contributed sponsorship and joined in with celebrations, helping develop good community relations and lasting connections with the people. (GCHS.)

Before the Cliff Jail was built, prisoners worked in the mines, but many escaped before they had completed their sentence. The Lesinskys paid local stonemason Margarito Varela to build a jail. Tradition says he celebrated the completion of the jail at a local saloon and was arrested for shooting up the place. He was thrown into the jail, becoming its first inmate. The jail was closed after the 1906 flood, when the inmates had to be rescued. A more suitable jail was built out of the flood zone. (RAC.)

As the towns were developed, various modes of transportation were used. The people traveled by trains, horses, wagons, boats, and automobiles. The one constant companion was the sturdy mule or burro. These animals were used from the beginning of mining operations and continued for a number of years, as depicted in this 1920s Clifton scene. (RAC.)

The street name on Clifton's Eastside was changed from Conglomerate Avenue to Gold Avenue in 1905, as the former name was felt to be outdated. Here is a scene on that street in 1914. Today, this street is called Park Avenue. (RAC.)

Clifton's Eastside is pictured in 1914, showing Devil's Canyon on the left. Today, this canyon is also known as the Lemon Squeezer. It has long been a challenge for daredevils to climb. The trail at the top leads to some excellent agate beds. Note the homes built into the side of the mountain. (RAC.)

The Bowman boys, Everett and Skeet, were on their way to Cheyenne, Wyoming, to compete in a big 1926 rodeo. Here, they are stopped on the road going into Clifton, probably checking on their horses and gear. It was a rough road between Clifton and Alpine, and they had 90 miles of the recently opened Coronado Trail in front of them. (GDH.)

In 1901, the Shannon Copper Company's smelter was built on Clifton's Cemetery Hill, later known as Shannon Hill. The company significantly boosted the economy and population of Clifton. In 1908, the company planted 200 cottonwood trees in the residence portion near the smelter, adding shade and beauty to the location. (GCHS.)

The freight depot for the Arizona & New Mexico Railway was built in 1913. The same construction firm that built the Arizona Copper Company manager's Eastside residence and passenger station also constructed this structure. Located just south of the passenger station, it was a key addition to railroad operations. The depot was damaged beyond repair in the 1983 flood, after which it was condemned and torn down. (GCHS.)

As seen here in 1925, the road from Clifton to Morenci wound its way up the mountainside along Chase Creek, with several hairpin turns. This road was known as Scotland's Curves, named for P.B. Scotland, a mine superintendent for the Arizona Copper Company who had a car accident on this road. (RAC.)

The Arizona Copper Company built this residence on Clifton's Eastside for general manager Norman Carmichael in 1913. The home had 20 rooms, of which six were bedrooms, each with a private bathroom. With a construction cost of $25,000, it was believed the company poured money into the project to avoid being taxed by the British government, since any funds not reinvested in the company were taxable. (GCHS.)

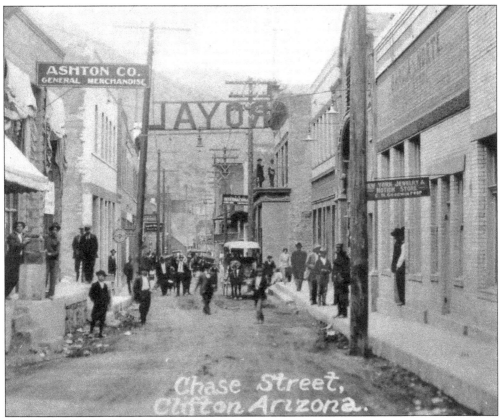

In this view looking south on Copper Avenue, or Chase Street at the time of this photograph, this section of town was as busy as big-city commercial districts. People hustling from store to store, horses and carriages clogging the street, sounds resonating from saloons and theaters, and the roar of the nearby Arizona Copper Company refinery all contributed to the cacophony of noise filling the mouth of Chase Creek Canyon. (GCHS.)

This view was taken high above Clifton in the 1940s. Slag was used as a berm along the length of the San Francisco River, all the way south to the base of Shannon Hill, as a way to protect the town from the destruction of floods. (GCHS.)

This early-1900s photograph of the San Francisco River was taken north of Potter's Ranch. Delbert Potter built a dam across the river around 1901 to provide irrigation for the 500 fruit trees on his property. He would often invite people from town to harvest the fruit. Potter was a pioneer in providing fresh water to Clifton for household use. (PW.)

Clifton and the Arizona Copper Company reduction works were bustling areas, as seen here on October 10, 1912. This facility had grown from a simple adobe smelter to a giant refinery and railroad hub. (GCHS.)

# Six

# MORENCI

Known as "the model mining camp of the Southwest," according to the *Arizona Bulletin Supplement* in 1903, Morenci was home to the Detroit Copper Company. The camp was originally known as Joy's Camp, named for Miles Joy, who led the surveying party in 1872. Later, the Detroit Copper Company took control of some of the major mines, and the community became known as Church's Camp, named after William Church. Maps of the day also labeled the area as Clifton Copper Mines, but in 1884, the town was officially named Morenci.

On Church's first visit to the camp, he and his companions camped under a tree near the future site of the plaza. During his years in Morenci, he would not permit removal of the tree, as it was a symbol of pride and endurance. Water was pumped from the San Francisco River and Eagle Creek for mining and domestic use. There were two rail inclines, the Fair Play and the Eagle. They descended Copper Mountain to ore bins, where the ore was loaded into railroad cars for transport to the smelters. The community of Longfellow was located just east of Morenci. The Longfellow Incline descended into Chase Creek Canyon, where ore was loaded onto railroad cars for transport to Clifton's Arizona Copper Company smelter.

The town was unique, being built in the bowl formed by numerous hills. Each hill was given an alphabetic designation, and residents identified with these sections of town. The A Hill was on the southwest side and held the courthouse and important water pipelines from Eagle Creek through the Pelican Tunnel. The AC Hill was on the southeast side and had a theater, Catholic church, saloons, bakery, and other businesses. The B Hill was on the west and had a tortilla shop, the town's water tanks, and a pipeline and road to Eagle Creek. The D Hill (Copper Mountain) was on the north and had a hospital, bank, two inclines, and many underground mines. The plaza had a train station, the Morenci Club, company stores, Hotel Morenci, schools, and a library. Early on, there were numerous trails and few roads. Mine blasts were heard day and night. The houses lining the hills in close proximity to one another made for a close-knit community.

In this 1880s photograph of early Morenci, many of the miners and their families still lived in tents. Eagle Mine, high up Copper Mountain, had an incline with ore bins at the mountain base on the left. At this time, the businesses were in the upper section of camp to the left. The saloons were a rowdy place, and soon people began to complain. The businesses were moved a short distance down Morenci Gulch. (GCHS.)

Morenci in 1892, was a fast-growing community. The Detroit Copper Company smelter on the right required a great deal of fuel in the form of mesquite trees, turned into charcoal. The hills of the district had been stripped of the trees very quickly. The bottom section of the picture, where the saloons and many of the businesses were, was known as Hell's Half Acre, a place that rivaled any Western town in the number of shootings, murders, and lawlessness. Here, gambling, saloons, and "soiled doves" parted miners from their hard-earned wages. A fire in 1897 wiped out the buildings, which led to the creation of New Town. (GCHS.)

As operations moved to open-pit mining in the late 1930s, a new smelter and concentrator were built in the Bunkers area, near the mouth of Morenci Canyon. This location provided a big area to build the refining facilities for ore coming from the mine. The smokestack, seen here under construction, would eventually top 600 feet. When production was in full swing, more miners and families began moving into the community. New housing can be seen in the upper left on Buena Vista Street. (GCHS.)

The Fairplay Shaft is shown with a large ore pile, probably from the nearby Arizona Central Mine, which was one of the first mines in Morenci. Mule teams with scrapers await their turn to drag ore to the loading chute. On the left side, a train has pulled below the chute and is being loaded, while another train down the canyon is waiting its turn. Eight scraper teams are working the huge pile. (AHS.)

As seen from AC Hill, the Morenci "M" stands guard over the town. The houses were owned by the occupants, but the land was owned by the companies. In 1908, rent for land owned by the Arizona Copper Company was raised to $1 per month. The money was used to fight typhoid fever that summer. (GCHS.)

In 1942, the Defense Plant Corporation came to Morenci to double the size of the secondary crusher, mill, and smelter to increase mine productivity in support of the war effort. Here, the road locally known as "10%" due to its steep grade has been rerouted to allow for new construction. (GCHS.)

Many heavy and very valuable copper anodes are being prepared for shipment on the Southern Pacific Railroad. Each anode weighed about 735 pounds and was approximately 98 percent copper. From here, the anodes were sent to El Paso, Texas, for further refining. (GCHS.)

Horses, burros, and donkeys were used to deliver goods around town, as seen here in 1916. Even when automobiles came to the district, horses were still a primary mode of transport because the early cars and trucks could not navigate the narrow and rough trails. The Detroit Copper Company's general office, the white building on the left, was completed in 1914 under the direction of G.M. Robinson, who was the chief engineer of the company. In addition to company offices, the building housed the superintendent of the Morenci Southern Railway. (GCHS.)

In this 1918 photograph, Tailings Dam foreman Fred Moore is checking the flow of tailings being deposited in the Plantsite area. Tailings, a mud-like waste material, is the milling remnant after ore has been crushed and valuable minerals have been extracted. Many sections of Clifton and Morenci are built on top of old tailings dumps. (CPM.)

Cock fights were very popular and drew large crowds. They generated a lot of money through placing bets. Here is such an event in Morenci in 1914. (RAC.)

Rails can be seen entering the Humboldt Mine. To the left is the Joy Shaft, and to the right, in the foreground, is the Arizona Copper Company store. The Humboldt Tunnel passed through Copper Mountain, which was one of the richest ore bodies ever found, and continued both underground and on the surface for approximately six miles. It carried ore from the Coronado mines west of Metcalf back to the concentrator in Morenci. (GCHS.)

At the turn of the century, Morenci was headed for a much needed face-lift. The Morenci Improvement Company was dedicated to upgrading the shacks and tents that dotted the hillsides into decent homes. The company was organized by Gordon McLean, who was the manager of the Detroit Copper Company, and showed the mine company's commitment to helping the people. (GDH.)

With not much room in town for construction, sometimes buildings of completely different purposes were in close quarters to each other, as was the case with the Detroit Copper Company metalurgical/assay building and the Morenci Jail (foreground) in 1914. (RAC.)

The receiving dock of the Detroit Copper Company store was always a busy scene. The Morenci Southern Railway train pulled alongside the dock to unload freight, which would be stored in the basement until inventoried and placed on the sales floor. The new railway depot is shown under construction in 1914. (RAC.)

The Longfellow Hospital, also known as the Arizona Copper Company Hospital in Morenci, was built in 1902. For a time, married mine employees were charged $5 a month for physician services, hospital, drug, and water fees. Employees who were single were charged $3.75 a month. (GCHS.)

Loop No. 4 of the Morenci Southern Railway was the biggest loop of the line. It was located in Morenci Canyon, south of the Detroit Copper Company slag dump. The trestles became too costly to maintain and in 1913 were replaced by switchbacks, which made the trip from Guthrie to Morenci longer. (GCHS.)

In later years, a few roads were created on the hills of Morenci to make traveling easier as the number of cars increased. One of the roads was known as Monster Road, seen here on the right. With its steep hill, it was aptly named since it could be a scary ride along this narrow road. Roads only wide enough for one vehicle had "pullout spots" for traffic going opposite directions. (GCHS.)

As open-pit operations got under way, equipment for such mining became necessary; however, development of the pit moved faster than that of the roads, which were often not ready to move equipment to complete the work. In this 1940s photograph, workers hoist a shovel up the canyon wall to get it in place. (GCHS.)

Charley's Auto Stage Company, seen here at a stop in New Town in 1914, serviced Clifton and Morenci. A car would depart from the Clifton Hotel, then stop in New Town before arriving at the Hotel Morenci. Using two cars, three round-trips were made daily. Each trip cost $3, or $1.50 for one way. (RAC.)

The Detroit Copper Company built its hospital in Morenci in 1902. It was heated by the boiler from inside the Arizona Central Mine at right. It had a medical and surgical ward, bathroom, operating room, attendant's room, and hardwood floors throughout the building, except for the operating room, where it had a cement floor. A cemetery was located on the hillside to the right. This mine was the first to be staked out and claimed in the district. (GCHS.)

A 1903 labor strike was one of the more brutal and bloody conflicts in the history of the district. Army troops and the Arizona Rangers were summoned to Morenci to keep the peace and ensure hostilities did not get out of hand. These troops are shown bivouacked in the plaza. (GCHS.)

The Longfellow Hotel, owned by the Arizona Copper Company, offered people a comfortable place to stay. With room accommodations often scarce in town, the company gladly welcomed guests into their hotel. The hotel served Morenci for many years, with social events booked months in advance. It was later renamed the Longfellow Inn. (RAC.)

The Arizona Copper Company rebuilt their mill in 1901 high above Chase Creek at Longfellow. This mill, along with the large smelter in Clifton that had five 200-ton furnaces, was capable of handling an impressive 1, 000 tons of ore per day. Compare that to the Morenci mine's recent record of one million tons mined in a single day. (GCHS.)

The Humboldt electric railway was completed in 1912 and was powered by direct current locomotives with power cables strung along the tunnel ceilings. It provided an efficient method to transport ore between the Coronado mine complex and No. 6 concentrator in Morenci. Utilizing the new system and eliminating the Coronado Incline saved a considerable amount of money for the company. (GCHS.)

In this view of Morenci in the 1960s, the familiar buildings of town are standing proud. The mine is closing in, and Copper Mountain is just a memory. (GCHS.)

Transportation between the towns was always a priority, and many businesses helped with that need. In addition to selling feed, the David M. Cansler Livery in Morenci provided stage service. At the time of this photograph, cars were in use, but some people still preferred horse-based transportation because of the rough and steep terrain. Floods would put the railroads out of service, so stages were used until the railroads could be fixed, proving their importance. The Detroit Copper Company office building, later known as the Fairplay School, is off in the distance. (RAC.)

As more miners came to work in the expanding open pit, the housing area of Plantsite was created for them and their families. To make buying goods easier, Phelps Dodge built a small mercantile (left), which served the families well for many years. Plantsite Elementary School (center) was established in 1944 so children could attend school close to home. Later, the school was renamed Longfellow. (GCHS.)

Law and order among the camps took men with nerves of steel; sometimes a quick gun draw would save their lives. Constable John Hoffman, posing in the plaza, served the people of Morenci in 1914. When the murderer of another lawman in Clifton was seen in Morenci a few days after the crime, Hoffman squared off against him and drew his gun faster than the culprit, killing him on the spot. (RAC.)

Narrow-gauge steam locomotives were used to transport ore from the Arizona Central and Fairplay Mines. The trains made connections with the No. 6 concentrator and the Longfellow Incline. (GCHS.)

The main route through town, and just about the only real street, was called Burro Alley. In the early days, the route from the top of the Longfellow Incline to the Arizona Copper Company Hospital was called Burro Trail. In 1941, this road and several other roads around town were improved and paved. (GCHS.)

The Morenci pit was lined with many miles of train tracks, which needed constant repair. Men of these crews were often called out for repairs at all hours, and no matter how bad the weather was, they completed their work so the business of mining could continue unabated. (GCHS.)

In this view looking down Morenci Canyon around 1905, four of the five loops for the Morenci Southern Railway are in view. The trestle in the left foreground is part of the railroad connecting the mines to the Detroit Copper Company smelter. (GCHS.)

As more people came to the mines and the population grew, another form of transportation was needed to get people and goods to Morenci. The narrow-gauge Morenci Southern Railway, which started at Guthrie 18 miles away, was an engineering marvel that served the district for over 20 years. The elevation gain of 1,400 feet from the San Francisco River to Morenci was a steep seven-mile climb, using a tunnel, bridges, and a series of loops and trestles. The first loop was situated near the river and required a tunnel, while the last four loops wound around Morenci

Canyon. Made from copper taken from the local mines, the last spike was driven on January 31, 1901. This trestle is located near the mouth of Morenci Canyon. On April 23, 1908, an outbound train wrecked on one of the loops when the air brakes failed. Both engineer and fireman jumped from the engine before it crashed into the canyon, taking three cars with it. Fortunately, the passenger car stayed on the tracks. No one was hurt in the accident. (RAC.)

In this aerial view of Morenci in the 1940s, town life and mining are closely tied. This photograph provides a spectacular view of the hills, businesses, and schools, while the mine looms large on the back side of Copper Mountain. (GCHS.)

The Detroit Copper Company No. 5 concentrator was located in Ryerson Canyon, with the West Yankee shaft headframe on the right. In the distance is the top of the Longfellow concentrator, which overlooked Chase Creek Canyon. On December 3, 1906, the tailings dam at this facility broke during a heavy rain and flooded Chase Creek with a torrent of mine waste and water, causing a large amount of destruction and loss of life. (RAC.)

The Detroit Copper Company smelter is seen in the foreground. On the hillside behind it is the Arizona Copper Company No. 6 mill. The close proximity of the immense facilities called for much cooperation between the companies. The town was a web of interconnected railroads between mines, concentrators, inclines, and the smelter. (GCHS.)

As early as 1913, the need for a separate place to house teachers was discussed. Teachers usually stayed under contract for only a few years and did not own a house. People in town often rented a room to a teacher, but this became problematic. The Teachers Court was built to give them comfortable lodging during their stay in town. (GCHS.)

Mules, burros, and horses were used throughout the district for all types of conveyance, from hauling groceries and lumber to firewood and ore cars. Seen in the Morenci plaza, these mules have large canvas bags on their pack saddles. They are probably being used to haul groceries from the Detroit Copper Company store. (RAC.)

This car and horse-drawn cart is pictured on the main road into Morenci in 1914. The use of automobiles was growing in the district but only on a limited basis. Horses, mules, and stage lines were used most often. The first automobile came to Clifton in 1908. (RAC.)

The Detroit Copper Company store was completed on March 3, 1901. As the pride of the town and company, it rivaled any store in bigger cities. The store was four stories high, and all the departments were connected via telephone. The basement had refrigerated rooms for cold storage, and a freight elevator serviced all floors. A wide range of items were sold, from hair pins to diamond jewelry and fine suits to work clothes. In 1906, the store expanded its offices and added plate glass showcases for merchandise. (GCHS.)

The Hotel Morenci, completed in 1902 for about $50,000, was a welcomed addition to the camp, ushering in a new era of luxury hotel accommodations. It was recognized by architectural engineers as one of the finest hotel structures in Arizona. On the first floor were the lobby, a bank, a post office, and lavatories. The second floor had offices, parlors, and a dining room. The third floor had rooms to accommodate up to 50 guests. Famous guests include Tom Mix and Fatty Arbuckle. A young Herbert Hoover stayed here on a visit while working for the Carlisle mines in New Mexico. (RAC.)

During World War II, women played a key role by working various jobs around the mine and smelter. These female workers are exiting the changing room on their way to the assigned work areas. When the war ended and men returned home, some women stayed in various positions for many years, working side by side with the men. Copper production was high and in great demand for the war effort, so the role women played during this period cannot be underestimated. (GCHS.)

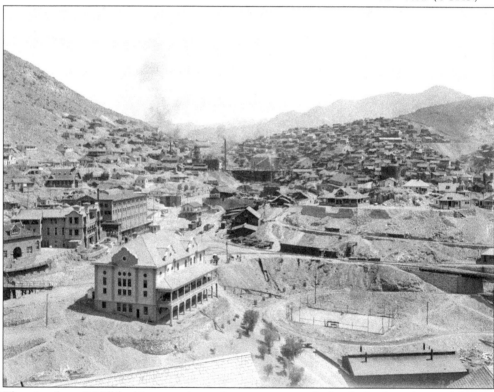

The view from B Hill looking east shows the amazing growth that had taken place in Morenci between 1884, when William Church moved his smelter here, and the early 1900s. This photograph was taken between 1902 and 1907. The Longfellow School, far left, is still a one-story structure. The Hotel Morenci, Detroit Copper Company store, Joy Shaft, Longfellow Hotel, Catholic church, Morenci Club, and managers' houses are new, impressive structures. Underground mining was located on Copper Mountain at left in the photograph. Also, mines were honeycombed below the town, causing the occasional cave-in and sink holes to suddenly appear. (GCHS.)

Narrow-gauge trains transported copper ore from the mines to the inclines. This early-1900s photograph was taken at the top of the Longfellow Incline. Miners hooked the ore cars to cables and lowered them to the railroad in Chase Creek Canyon for shipment to the Clifton smelters. (GCHS.)

Morenci was not exempt from crime and other dramatic events. The Holy Cross Catholic Church was the site of anarchists attempts to destroy it with dynamite. In the early hours of August 2 and September 14, 1913, people were awoken by the sound and vibration of intense explosions that shook the camp. Luckily, the priest happened to be sleeping in a different part of the church each time. Prior to these attempts, the priest's home had been dynamited twice, so he moved into the church, only to have the would-be murderers attempt to take his life there. In this photograph from February 6, 1914, the church is still being repaired. (GCHS.)

The Detroit Copper Company store served the people well for many years. The ice plant, to the left of the store, provided much-needed ice for the community, as well as for the goods being stored in the basement that needed to be chilled until purchase. (PW.)

The Arizona Copper Company's No. 6 concentrator, built by the Warden Allen Company, is seen under construction on February 14, 1906. Ore was transported through a series of tunnels via the Humboldt electric railway to this mill for processing. A hoist shaft at the top of the facility raised the ore from the tunnel 400 feet to the primary crusher. (GCHS.)

Moving day in Morenci required ingenious minds and sometimes strong backs. The hills were crisscrossed with trails that could not accommodate vehicles. This gentleman has packed household items on his back to move them to new accommodations. (RAC.)

Chihuahua Hill in the distance was so named because, at one time, most of the people living there were from Chihuahua, Mexico. The name later changed to B Hill. The houses on the steep hills of early-day Morenci were interconnected by trails. Roads would be built in later years when cars were more prevalent. The road to Eagle Creek is on the far right, leading over the hill. (GCHS.)

The men of the Humboldt Mine at Longfellow, like all miners, were a hardy bunch. Tough and dangerous conditions above and belowground were no place for weak men. The Humboldt Tunnel and rail system ran north from Morenci, through Copper Mountain, then crossed a series of trestles and tunnels, ending at the Coronado Incline. (PW.)

Open-pit mining was much different from the underground days, requiring new techniques and equipment. Here, the No. 13 drill at the upper left, along with the No. 13 shovel, work together to break up the rock and load it into the dump trucks. Each level in the pit bench was 50 feet high. The drills made a number of holes that were then filled with explosives and detonated, fracturing the rock. This was a 24-hour operation, therefore, the pit grew quickly. Explosives were set off each day at 3:30 p.m. The bulldozer at right works to assist the big pit shovels and keep the area clear in order for the equipment to move freely. (GCHS.)

# Seven

# METCALF

Named for the Metcalfe brothers, the town of Metcalf was in Chase Creek Canyon and Coronado Gulch, northeast of Morenci. "The city with a past," as labeled by the October 9, 1929, *El Paso Evening Post*, was first settled in 1872, and at its peak, the town population was about 5,000 people. The post office was established in 1899 and was discontinued in 1936. Residents traveled numerous trails and on the Coronado Railroad. In the early 1900s, a bumpy road was built from Clifton to Metcalf. The town's jail was in an old abandoned mine tunnel. Being very unsanitary, a more adequate jail was later constructed.

The town was described in the August 8, 1907, *Copper Era* as "a little hill city entirely surrounded by mines." The Shannon, Metcalf, Wilson, King, Coronado, and Queen Inclines came down the mountain sides around Metcalf, providing a link from the underground mines to the railroads, which transported ore to the smelters. The Shannon Copper Company's mines were on Shannon Ridge, east of Metcalf. Ore was shipped to the company's smelter in Clifton. The Detroit Copper Company had mines in the area and shipped their ore to Morenci for processing, while the Arizona Copper Company sent their ore to mills and smelters in both Morenci and Clifton. There were other companies operating in the area, such as the Santa Rosa Copper Company, the Standard Copper Company, and the Stevens mines. All prospered from the rich ore bodies.

Metcalf had many attractions. People came to the area for sightseeing. Traveling up the Coronado Railroad from Clifton provided spectacular mountain views. The game of baseball came to Metcalf in 1910. The team competed against Clifton's Greys and Cubs and Morenci's Independents. Residents enjoyed events at Juarez Hall for many years. This was a great convenience as opposed to traveling to Morenci or Clifton for entertainment. The town lived and died with the successes and failures of the mines that dotted the surrounding mountains. When the underground mines started to close, people began to move away. The town was one of the biggest in Graham and later Greenlee County.

The BBB store and the White Owl saloon complex in Metcalf also housed a hotel. It was a very important stop along the Coronado Railroad. A fire in April 1909 caused $25,000 worth of damage and destroyed these structures, but they were soon rebuilt and businesses thrived. This section of Metcalf was known as Katzville, since Henry Katz owned these buildings. BBB stood for *Bueno, Barato, y Bonito* ("Good, Cheap, and Pretty"). (GCHS.)

The district's impressive inclines required massive cable systems. Taken from inside the building of the Shannon Incline hoist, this view shows these cables in action, as well as the machinery needed to lower the heavy cars loaded with ore down the mountain to the waiting trains. The inclines were very steep, so the cables needed to be strong and in good condition. (GCHS.)

The mountainous region of the district led to numerous engineering feats. Many sections of railroad traveled over trestles, bridges, and tunnels. The Shannon Tunnel up Chase Creek to the Shannon Incline in Metcalf was one of many tunnels servicing the railroads. (GCHS.)

Smaller companies tried to make it easier to produce copper. For example, the Santa Rosa Copper Company built its smelter near Metcalf. In 1910, there were plans to build a smelter near the Shannon Mine for the Arizona, Detroit, and Shannon Copper Companies. Arizona marketed through United Metals, Detroit through Phelps, Dodge & Company, and Shannon through American Metal. (GCHS.)

The bins at left were used for ore coming down from the Wilson and Metcalf Inclines. The Arizona Copper Company operated the Coronado Railroad, whose rails are seen in the photograph. They hauled the ore to the refinery in Clifton, seven miles down the canyon. There were more ore bins up the canyon. (GCHS.)

Central Metcalf was filled with houses and businesses built in close proximity. The railroad trestle at center was part of the Shannon Railway, which ran along the west side of Chase Creek Canyon. The Coronado Railroad tracks can be seen running through the bottom of the canyon, close to the stores and residences. The prominent three-story white building at center is Metcalf High School. The Coronado Incline is visible in the distance. (GCHS.)

In Metcalf, structures were built wherever a grip on the hillside or creek bottom could be found. As seen, many had stilt supports and retainer walls, and most had no yards. A nighttime visit to the outhouse could be a hazardous endeavor. (GCHS.)

Engines No. 2, No. 5, and No. 7 of the Arizona Copper Company were abandoned at the top of the Coronado Incline when mining operations ceased in 1922. In the 1990s, they were recovered and refurbished for display. There are many tales of tough hikes to see the engines as they sat alone near the old mountain town of Coronado. They were a great reminder of the glory days in the district when these small, tough engines pulled cars filled with copper. (GCHS.)

The Shannon Copper Company store (far left) was relocated from the top of Shannon Ridge to the base of the incline in 1905. More families were moving down from the mountain, so the company recognized a store was needed at the bottom. From this point at the bottom of the Shannon Incline, ore was loaded onto trains for transport to the smelter on Shannon Hill in Clifton. On January 13, 1914, a new sight and sound was witnessed in Metcalf—the automobile. The road had recently been widened, and when the first automobile rumbled into town with the driver honking the horn, people gathered around to marvel at the machine and hear the driver's tale of his trip from Clifton. (GCHS.)

Underground mining techniques evolved throughout the years from the simple pickax, pry bars, shovels, and hand drills to hydraulic drills and railcars to haul away the ore. The mountains around Metcalf were surrounded by numerous mines and tunnels. In this photograph, a crew drills the tunnel's face, preparing it for explosives. It was hard, dangerous work that occasionally resulted in cave-ins. Miners had to work safely and have nerves of steel. (GCHS.)

Metcalf had many sturdy rock walls that supported railroads, roadways, homes, mine structures, and businesses. Here, 10 homes cling to the canyon walls. Note the extensive Y-supports under the large residence at left. (GCHS.)

The railroads in Metcalf were in close quarters with the early trails and narrow roads along Chase Creek Canyon. Accidents between the trains and horse and burro traffic were common, not to mention the floodwater that damaged the trails and tracks. In 1907, the county board of supervisors allocated money from the high taxes residents of the town were already paying to improve the roads. Soon, bridges and rock retaining walls were being constructed. These additions not only addressed important safety concerns, but were also aesthetically pleasing. (GCHS.)

It does not appear that electric service has reached these residences in Metcalf. Note the clotheslines on the homes at left. The work of washing clothes was done by hand, then hung to dry on rope or wire lines strung on porches. The bridge crosses Chase Creek, which was usually a mere trickle. However, with rainstorms in the mountains above Metcalf, the mild-mannered creek could turn into a raging monster of floodwater. (GCHS.)

The Matilda Mine headframe and buildings were prominent among the structures in Coronado. It was the main mine of the Coronado Group. Belowground at this point, a number of tunnels, levels, and drifts branched out in different directions to penetrate rich ore bodies. The famous 3,200-foot-long Coronado Incline, one mile east of town, served these mines. Its ore cars were lowered and raised on the incline by cable. (GCHS.)

The high elevations, majestic mountains and canyons, and spectacular views made Metcalf a well-known destination for travelers. The passenger train of the Coronado Railroad would often stop so riders could disembark to capture pictures that would be cherished for a lifetime. Here, the railroad's long-serving engineer George Gamble is stopped along the route with his sightseeing passengers enjoying the trip. (WRR.)

In 1913, Oliver Risdon built a new pool hall, shown at right. He is standing on the steps of his new Metcalf photography studio. Risdon came to Clifton around 1900 and initially had his studio on the Eastside. After a flood damaged his property, Risdon relocated his studio to Copper Avenue (Chase Creek) around 1915. In 1921, he moved to Los Angeles, California, but came back in 1925. He also had studios in Morenci and Safford. In 1940, the Clifton studio was sold to Frank Gabusi, and Risdon passed away shortly thereafter. Many of the photographs that have survived throughout the years are his. They provide a great historical record of the district. (GCHS.)

The Shannon Incline north of Metcalf was said to be the steepest incline in the world. Ore was lowered down to awaiting trains of the Shannon Railroad to be transported to Clifton for processing. People who lived at the top of the incline either took the trail up and around the mountain to get home, or if they were lucky, they caught a ride in an empty ore car to the top. (GCHS.)

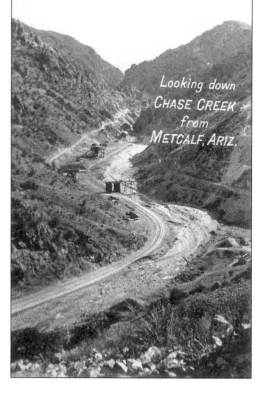

Looking down CHASE CREEK from METCALF, ARIZ.

One of the lesser known inclines was the Queen, serviced by the ore bins in the foreground. It was about halfway between Metcalf and the Longfellow Incline and was owned by the Arizona Copper Company. The ore bins in the distance were for the Standard Mine. The road in the canyon would later be called the Coronado Trail, part of Highway 666. Clifton is down the canyon, Morenci over the mountain to the right, and Metcalf up the canyon to the left. (GCHS.)

Looking north along Chase Creek, the upper rails belong to the Shannon Copper Company, the lower is part of the Coronado Railroad. The Shannon-Arizona Railway was opened on February 25, 1910. Before the railway opened, the company transported its ore to Clifton on the Coronado Railroad, which was operated by the Arizona Copper Company, but costs were high and the constant floods along the creek hindered shipments. To solve this problem, the company built its railroad high along the west side of Chase Creek, eventually leading to the summit called Shannon Junction near the location of the Conoco gas station in present-day Morenci, then down the mountainside above Shannon Hill to the smelter. (GCHS.)

This harrowing view down the Shannon Incline puts its steepness into perspective. At over 900 feet long, it was believed to be the steepest incline in existence. Note the numerous trails on the mountainside across Chase Creek Canyon, which provided access to the many mines in the area. (GCHS.)

From the top of the Shannon Incline is a great view of the Shannon townsite in the distance and the entrance to the Boulder Tunnel on the right. A mule pulling ore cars can be seen near the mine portal. Just out of sight on the left was a large corral where mules and horses were kept. There were no locomotives in the Shannon Mines, so these animals were used to move ore, as well as supplies and mining equipment. (GCHS.)

The King was another incline that serviced the underground mines near Metcalf. The bottom of the incline crossed over a bridge and through the 1,500-foot-long Torpedo (or King Tunnel), then connected to the Wilson Incline, which lowered the ore to the Arizona Copper Company bins and trains in Metcalf. (GCHS.)

The Arizona Copper Company hospital in Metcalf opened on February 15, 1908. A Miss Clark came from the company's hospital in Clifton to be the head nurse. It had three large wards, a large bathroom, an operating room, a kitchen, and a bedroom for the nurses. The building had steam heat and gas lighting. Before the hospital was built, doctors and nurses were kept busy traveling from house to house to perform their duties. Within a six-week period in 1907, five sets of twins were born, adding to the excitement around the camp. (GCHS.)

Operations inside the underground mines was dangerous and tough work. Here, miners at the mine face are using mallets and hand drills to make holes in the rock for dynamite charges. The loose rock will then be sorted and taken to the surface in man- and mule-powered ore cars. This scene is from the Wilson Mine around 1900. (RAC.)

In the period before open-pit mining, the district was dotted with underground mines, with over 100 throughout the area. This photograph is an excellent example of the caving technique used in many of the underground mines. When a rich lode of ore was found, it was mined out, and empty spaces, or caves, were left, making some mine interiors look like Swiss cheese. This method could be very dangerous because support timbering was often impossible. Cave-ins were very common. (PW.)

Risdon's photography studio can be seen at the lower right, and the Shannon Railroad trestle, in the background, spans the mouth of Coronado Gulch. The Coronado Railroad is at the lower left. The playground for the elementary school is also at the lower left, offering students an up-close view of passing trains. (GCHS.)

In 1907, a dead man was found on the main road along Chase Creek on the south side of town. It was determined that he had died of heart failure. He was buried in the Metcalf cemetery with the following epitaph on his gravestone: "Here lying prone beneath this stone, is Jose Maria Carrion. He had an attack of cardiac that laid him flat on his back. Within this hole rests his mold, but God knows where he sent his soul." In 1952, as the open-pit mine grew in size, the graves were moved near the present site of Morenci. (GCHS.)

In this view looking south along Chase Creek, Metcalf is full of activity. The large buildings on the left are the elementary school, then the Arizona Copper Company store. Metcalf, like Morenci, had no roads on the hillsides, so houses were connected by trails. (GCHS.)

Along the east side of Chase Creek and on the north side of Metcalf were the Wilson (left) and the Metcalf Inclines. The inclines were owned by the Arizona Copper Company, and the ore was sent to Clifton for processing via the Coronado Railroad. (GCHS.)

The Standard Mines south of Metcalf were great copper producers for many years. The ore bins pictured here were close to the mines. Ore was dumped into the chute at the top, then carried on a 3000-foot-long tram to ore bins on the east side of Chase Creek. From there, it was transported by train to the Shannon smelter in Clifton. (GCHS.)

# *Eight*

# REBIRTH

A painful reality of expansion is sometimes towns in close proximity to the mine face inevitable extinction. When mining of the Clay ore body in Morenci's pit started in 1937, waste rock was dumped into Chase Creek Canyon, covering much of Metcalf. In the 1980s, people came to witness the destruction of the last buildings in Morenci and maybe take a souvenir. It was difficult to watch childhood memories being wiped away. Driving up the main road was like visiting a war zone, with debris and rocks strewn across the street.

The pit grew fast and began encroaching on Morenci proper in the 1950s, continuing through the early 1980s. Morenci Hospital was taken down brick by brick and moved to a new site in 1969. The building's materials were donated to the detention center at Fort Grant in Arizona. The Metcalf pit expansion eventually merged with the Morenci open pit. Through the 1980s, only a few foundations, inclines, pieces of abandoned mining equipment, and sections of the original Coronado Trail could be seen. During the era, families dismantled their homes and rebuilt in other locations. The housing site of Stargo was fully dismantled and, like Old Morenci, buried under massive leach fields where copper and heavy metal extracts are recovered. After a life of approximately 110 years, the old town ceased to exist.

The Metcalfe, Lesinsky, and Stevens brothers would be amazed if they could visit the area today and observe its massive changes. The towns of Clifton and Morenci have remained an integral part of the mine's success. Clifton, though much diminished by floods and strikes, is making a comeback. Many of the old buildings are being revitalized, and new businesses are setting up shop. A new Morenci was built, and a modern high school was completed for $10.3 million in 1982. The mines have now flourished for over 140 years, providing copper and precious metals to the world. People still migrate here for good-paying jobs. Of the old towns, only memories, pictures, and stories remain, but they will always be in the hearts and souls of its people and an important part of Arizona history.

The Morenci pit looms large over the vestiges of the community in 1969. Copper Mountain is gone, and the blasting was so close, the force of the blast shook buildings and nerves. (GCHS.)

The shops, trucks, and equipment of modern mining have replaced the homes and businesses of central Metcalf, as seen in this photograph from September 1988. (RAC.)

The small building at center was part of the Phelps Dodge employment office, which is one of the last buildings visible as Old Morenci is buried during mining operations in September 1988. Many of the Phelps Dodge employees who drove the dump trucks or dismantled the buildings were graduates of Morenci High School, and as such, they had a hard time dealing with the fact that they were helping to bury the town they loved. The area of the vanished town of Metcalf is seen at center in the far distance. (RAC.)

In this haunting scene of Old Morenci's last days, around 1980, the town seems to be part of a dream. Gone are the children at the school, patrons at the Morenci Club, shoppers at the stores, and moviegoers at the Royal Theater. (CM.)

Shown in the late 1980s, Morenci nears its end as it is filled in with mine waste, rock, and dirt. The high school and auditorium at right and the cafeteria at upper left were some of the last buildings remaining before being completely buried. (GCHS.)

Construction for the housing development of Stargo is well under way in this image from September 10, 1943. With the Coronado homes in the foreground, tiny trailers line the far hillside, which housed the hundreds of workers who were building the stucco houses. (PW.)

Houses were built in the Plantsite area when more miners came to the district beginning in the 1940s. The picture above shows the houses of Site 1 under construction, with Aristata Drive on the left and Palo Verde Road on the right. Acacia and Columbine Roads will be built over the hill to the right and Chaparral Road to the south. Site 2 is under construction below, with Oleander Road on the right and Yucca Avenue on the left. Manzanita Road is angling off to the right, and Ocotillo Road is branching off Yucca Avenue to the left. Paradise Lane would later be built off the slope to the left. (Both, PW.)

The new 42-bed Morenci Hospital in Plantsite was built for $1.8 million in the late 1960s. The town was expanding rapidly so this facility offered patients a modern and convenient place to receive care. (GCHS.)

The need for additional housing was realized, and new residences were built on the site of the former Copper Verde Park in Clifton. East Plantsite sits on the hill in the distance, and a huge ore pile being leached for copper covers the old Stargo location and towers over Square Butte. (HG.)

In this view looking north toward the ever-encroaching mine, Morenci is viewed from Cholla Road in September 2014. A new era of mining is well under way as the town looks ahead to a bright future while honoring and remembering its historic past. (RAC.)

South Clifton and Shannon Hill are viewed from Mares Bluff in September 2014. As unique today as ever, the town of Clifton continues to welcome new residents and businesses as it restores and preserves its historic buildings and treasured memories. (AS.)

Visit us at
arcadiapublishing.com

Printed in the USA
CPSIA information can be obtained
at www.ICGtesting.com
LVHW081957120923
757853LV00009B/596

9 781531 678326